FOOTBALL

by Brendan Flynn

Early Encyclopedias

An Imprint of Abdo Reference
abdobooks com

abdobooks.com

Published by Abdo Reference, a division of ABDO, PO Box 398166, Minneapolis, Minnesota 55439.
Copyright © 2024 by Abdo Consulting Group, Inc. International copyrights reserved in all countries.
No part of this book may be reproduced in any form without written permission from the
publisher. Early Encyclopedias™ is a trademark and logo of Abdo Reference.

052023
092023

THIS BOOK CONTAINS
RECYCLED MATERIALS

Editor: Charlie Beattie
Series Designers: Candice Keimig, Joshua Olson

Library of Congress Control Number: 2022949126

Publisher's Cataloging-in-Publication Data

Names: Flynn, Brendan, author.
Title: Football / by Brendan Flynn
Description: Minneapolis, Minnesota: Abdo Reference, 2024 | Series: Early sports encyclopedias |
    Includes online resources and index.
Identifiers: ISBN 9781098291280 (lib. bdg.) | ISBN 9781098277468 (ebook)
Subjects: LCSH: Football--Juvenile literature. | American football--Juvenile literature. | Team
    sports--Juvenile literature. | Sports--History--Juvenile literature. | Encyclopedias and
    dictionaries--Juvenile literature.
Classification: DDC 796.03--dc23

CONTENTS

Football is the most popular sport in the United States. Starting in the fall, high school players all over the country play on Friday nights. College football teams take the field on Saturdays. The National Football League (NFL) has games multiple times a week. Millions of fans watch games in stadiums and on TV every week.

Football is a fast-paced game. It can be very dangerous. Players are athletic and tough. Football is still played mostly by boys and men. Women started to play the sport more in the 2000s.

The Ball

A football is shaped like an oval with pointy ends. Most footballs are made of leather panels stitched together over a rubber bladder. The top of the ball has thick stitches called laces. When players throw the ball, they usually put their fingers on the laces.

Basics of the Game

A football game is played between two teams. Most of the time, each team has 11 players on the field at once.

One side is on offense. Players on offense try to score points. Whichever team has the most points when the time clock runs out wins.

The other side is on defense. Players try to stop the offense. They do this by tackling the player with the ball. The defense can also try to take the ball away from the offense. Any takeaway can be returned for a touchdown. That is one way a defense can score points.

Every team also has a special teams lineup. Special teams players are on the field when the ball is being kicked. Some special teams plays are field goals or extra points after touchdowns. Other plays are punts or kickoffs. On these plays, one team kicks the ball to the other.

The Tampa Bay Buccaneers, *left*, and Washington Commanders line up for a play.

Downs and Scoring

The game begins when one team kicks off to the other. Teams then take turns on offense and defense. The offense has four plays—also called downs—to move the ball 10 yards. If it gets 10 or more yards, the offense earns a new set of four downs.

The offense's goal is to score points. Teams get six points for a touchdown. That's when a player brings the ball into the opponent's end zone.

A marker lets players know what down it is.

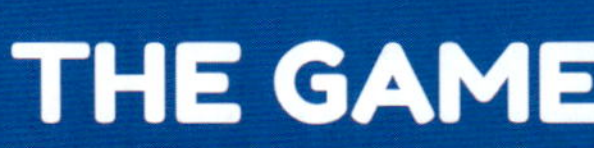

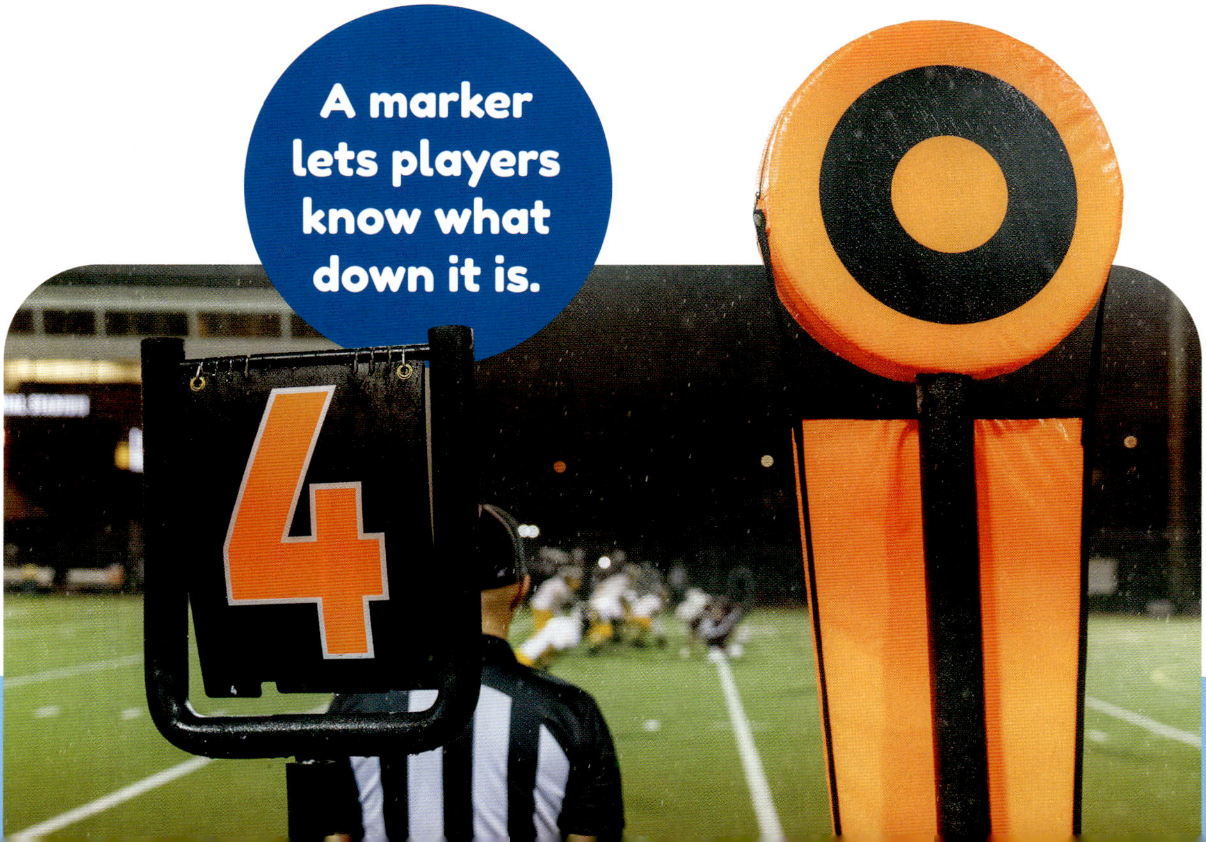

Teams can also try for a field goal. Kicking the ball through the goalposts at the end of the field earns three points.

After a scoring play, the team that scored kicks off. Then the other team's offense gets its turn to try to score.

FUN FACT!

After a touchdown, the scoring team can kick the ball through the goalposts for one point. It can also run a play from near the goal line. If the player with the ball reaches the end zone, that's worth two points.

The Field

A football field is 100 yards long. That's the distance from goal line to goal line. Each end zone is 10 yards long. So the playing field is actually 120 yards long. It is 53.3 yards wide from sideline to sideline. Some fields are real grass. Many others are artificial turf.

The field has many markings painted on it. That way players, referees, and fans know exactly where the ball is on the field.

Canadian Football

The Canadian Football League (CFL) was formed in 1958. Its playing field is 110 yards long and 65 yards wide. The 55-yard line is the center of the field. And the end zones are 20 yards deep.

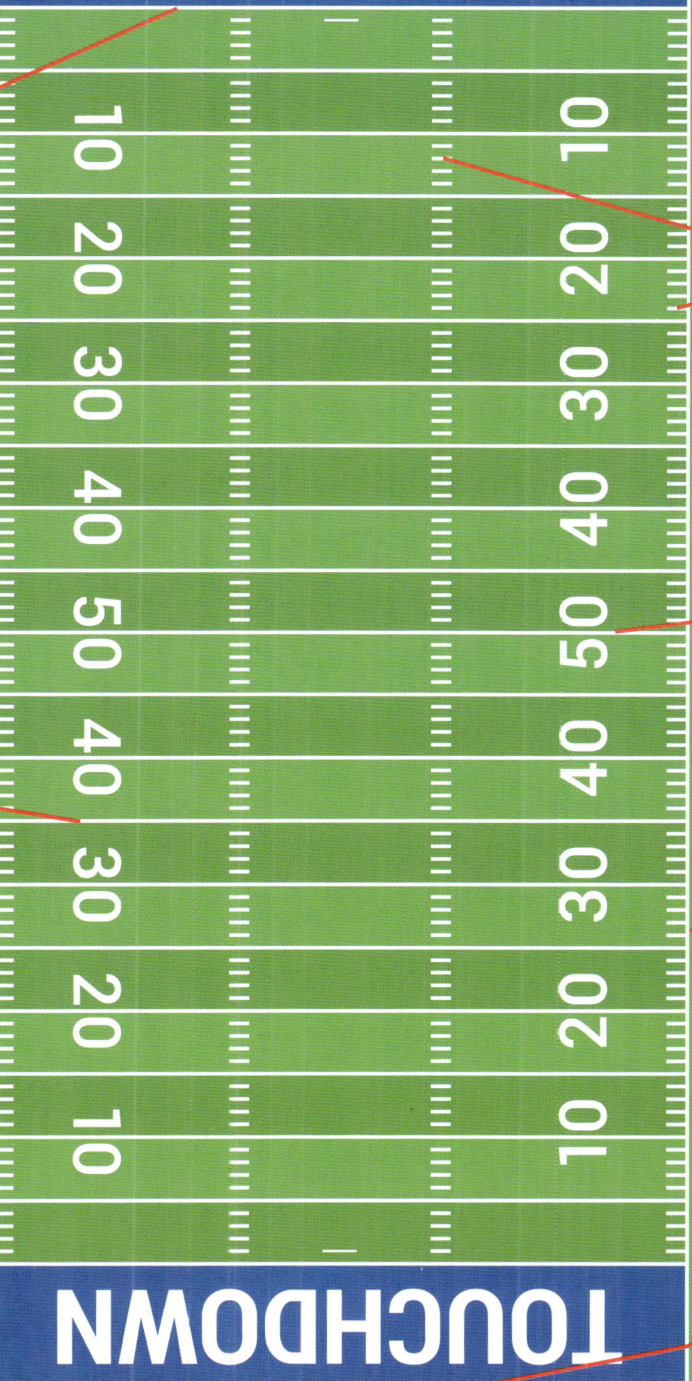

end zone
goal line
TOUCHDOWN
hash marks
10
20
30
40
50
50
40
30
20
10
50-yard line
yard line
sideline
TOUCHDOWN
goalpost

Uniforms and Equipment

Football is a physical game. Players need a lot of equipment to help protect themselves from injuries. Shoulder pads, hip pads, thigh pads, and knee pads are all part of most players' uniforms.

The most important piece of equipment is the helmet. Football helmets have a hard plastic shell. Inside, special padding protects the player's head. The helmet also has a hard face mask.

Football players wear matching jerseys, pants, and socks. Football cleats have plastic studs on the sole to help provide grip when running.

Football Uniform

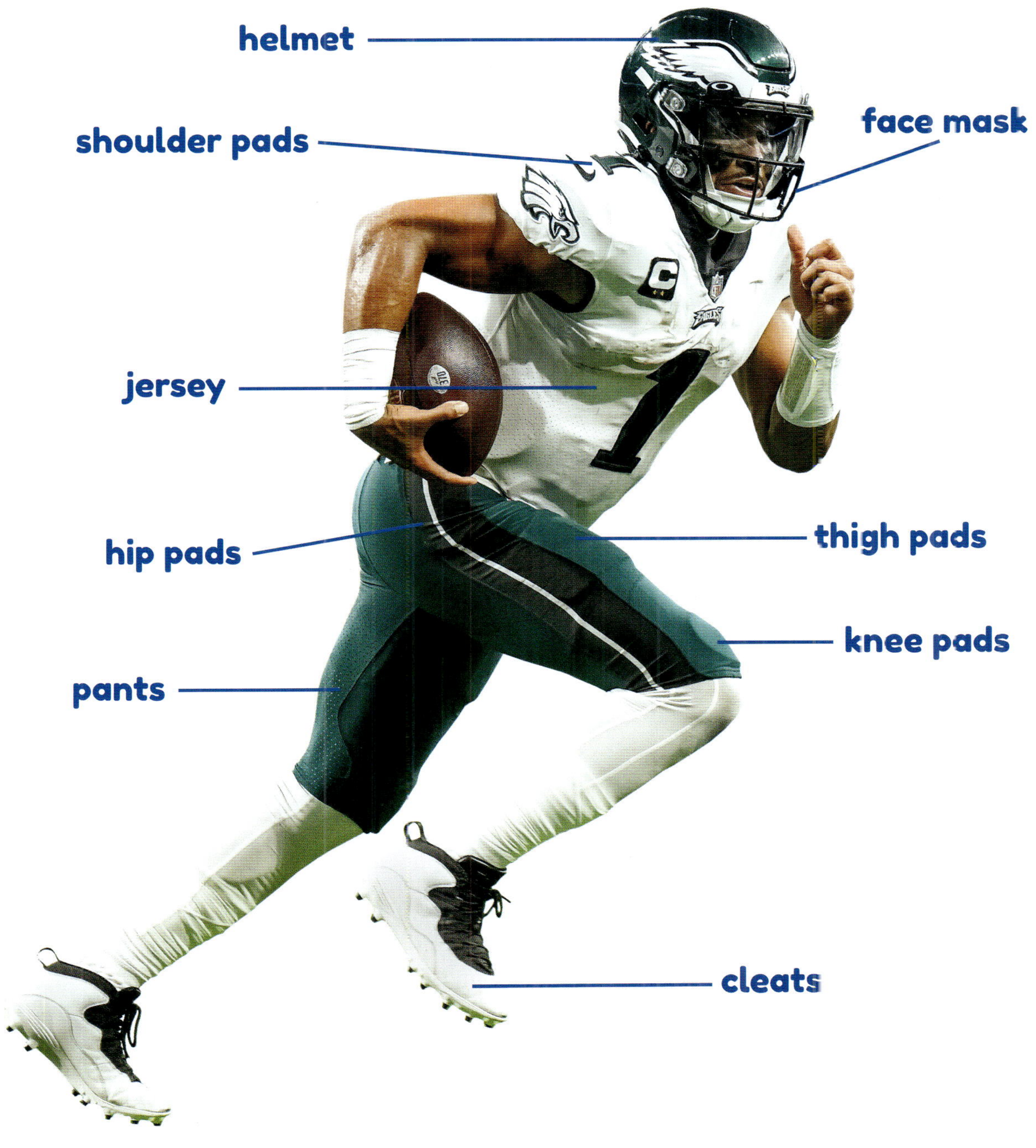

Offense

The job of the offense is to get the ball down the field and score points. An offense can move the ball in two ways. It can either run or pass the ball.

For running plays, the quarterback can hand off or toss the ball to a teammate. Sometimes the quarterback keeps the ball and runs himself.

Passing allows an offense to quickly move the ball long distances. A quarterback can attempt a forward pass only from behind the line of scrimmage. A receiver must catch the ball and land inbounds for the pass to be complete.

Blocking

Blocking is the foundation of an offense. This is when a player uses his body to stop an opponent from moving. Players can use their arms to help push defenders while blocking. But they cannot grab on to an opponent. If they do, it is a penalty called holding.

The linemen are an offense's most important blockers.

An offensive lineman for the Arizona Cardinals, *left*, makes a block during an NFL game.

They block to give the quarterback time on passing plays. On running plays, linemen try to create holes for the runner to burst through. All offensive players must be able to block, however. They might be asked to block on any play in which they are not carrying the ball.

Defense

The defense tries to stop the other team from scoring. It tries to get the ball back to its own offense. Many players have to work together to do this.

The main positions on defense are linemen, linebackers, and defensive backs. Defensive linemen try to stop running backs at or behind the line of scrimmage. They also try to tackle the quarterback on passing plays.

Linebackers play in the middle of the defense. They defend both running backs and receivers

Linemen:	Linebackers:	Defensive backs:
DT defensive tackle	MLB middle linebacker	CB cornerback
NT nose tackle	OLB outside linebacker	S safety
DE defensive end	ILB inside linebacker	

Defensive Formations

going out for passes. Defensive backs play the farthest away from the ball. Their main job is to cover receivers.

Tackling

There are many ways an offensive play can end. The most common way is for the ballcarrier to be tackled. A tackle is a physical move to bring down an opponent. Once that opponent is on the ground, the play is over.

Plays can also end when a player goes out of bounds. One big difference between an offensive player being tackled and going out of bounds is the clock. The clock stops when a player steps out of bounds. However, it keeps running after a tackle. Late in games, offensive players often try to run out of bounds to stop the clock. That helps the offense run more plays.

FUN FACT!

If a defense tackles a ballcarrier in his own end zone, that's called a safety. The defensive team gets two points.

Two defensive players close in to tackle a ballcarrier.

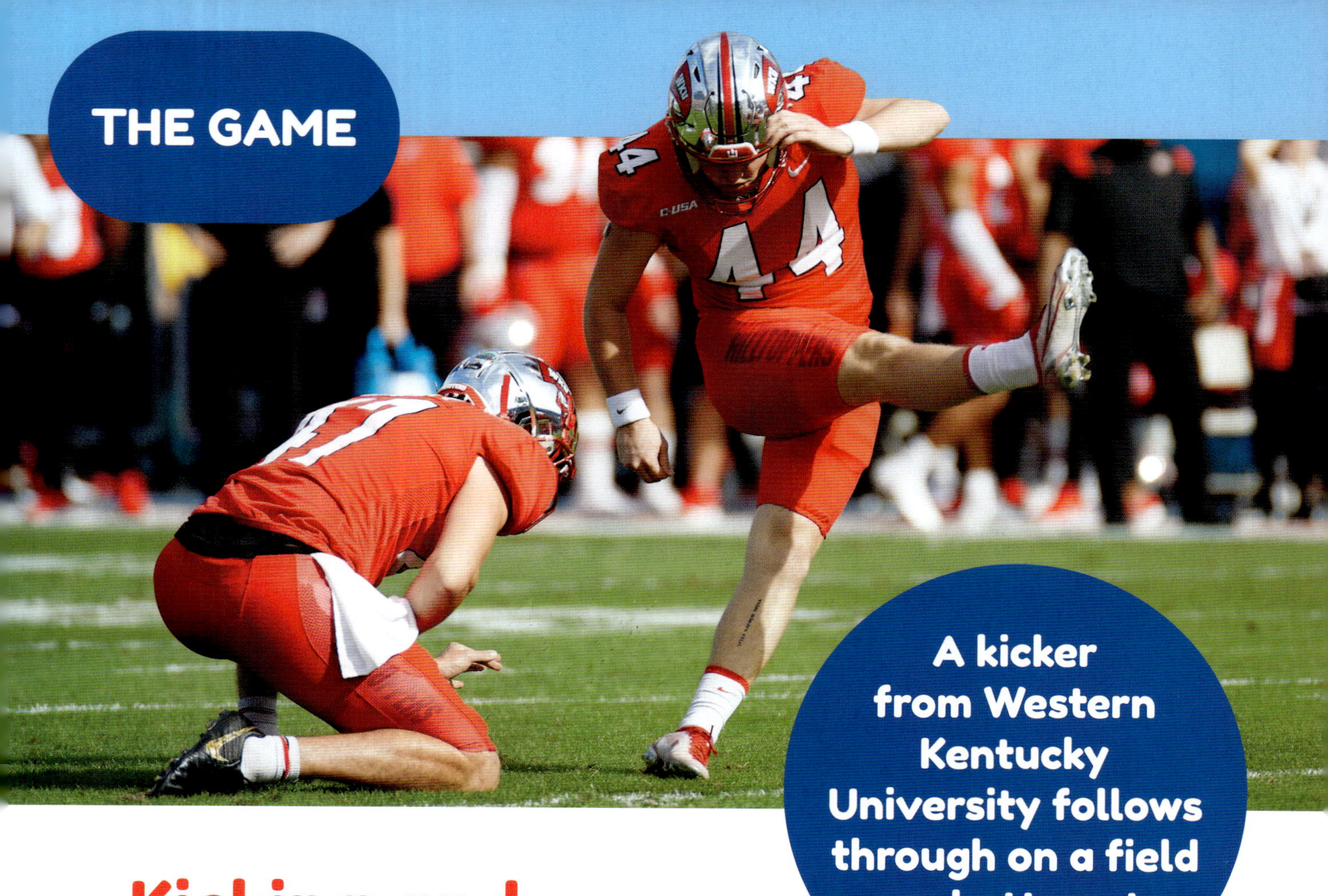

Kicking and Special Teams

Special teams are also a part of the game. Special teams plays are any play that involves a kick. That includes extra points, field goals, punts, and kickoffs.

An offense that is unlikely to score a touchdown can kick a field goal. The kicker tries to kick the ball between the uprights at the back of the end zone. A field goal is worth three points. An extra point works the same way. It comes after a touchdown.

Punts and kickoffs give the ball back to the other team. The goal of a punt is to get the ball as far down the field as possible. Kickoffs happen after scoring plays. A kicker boots the ball off a tee. Then his teammates race down to try and tackle the return man.

Passing

Quarterbacks need strong arms to throw the ball a long way. They also need to be accurate with their passes. A few steps are important to throw the ball well.

Most quarterbacks grip the ball with their fingers over the ball's laces. When a quarterback is ready to throw, he points his front shoulder at his target. The he shifts his weight to his back foot, below his throwing arm.

Former Duke University quarterback Daniel Jones sets up for a pass by gripping the ball on its laces.

BC Lions quarterback Michael Reilly, *right*, steps toward his target while following through on a pass.

He takes a step toward his target and brings the ball up behind his ear. He takes a stride, raising his throwing arm to bring the ball forward.

Then the quarterback releases the throw. He snaps his wrist to spin the ball and give the throw more power. He finishes his motion by following through with his arm.

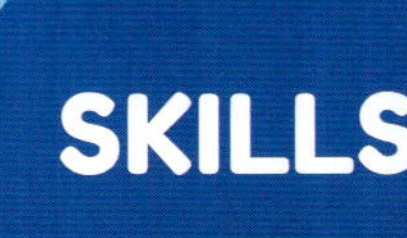

Receiving

Catching a football the right way takes a lot of practice. Players may want to pin the ball to their chests. But the best receivers learn to catch with their hands away from their bodies.

A receiver's hand position is important. He holds his hands in front of him with his palms facing away. His thumbs should be touching and so should his index fingers. This will make a diamond shape.

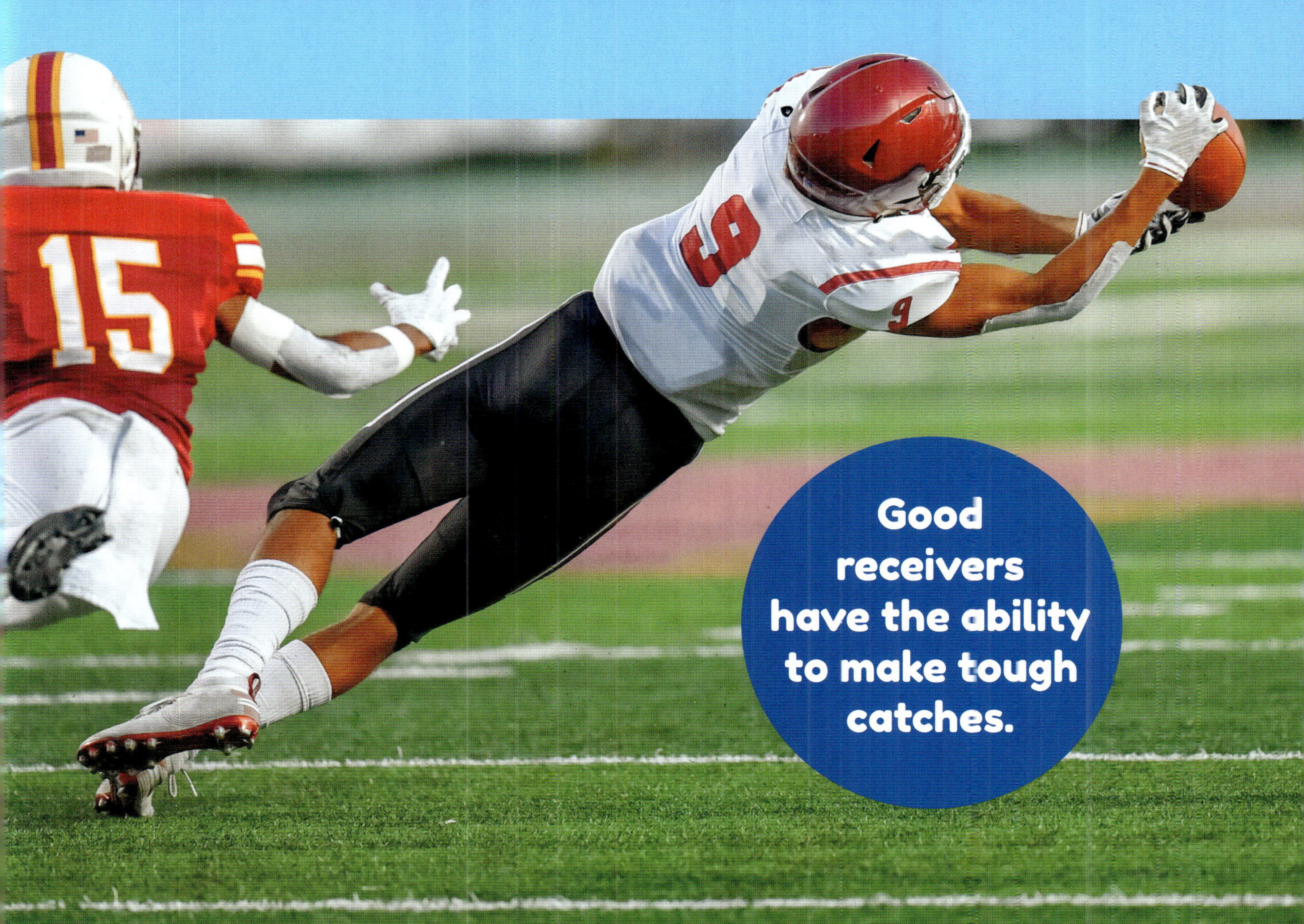

That's where the tip of the ball should land when he makes a catch.

A receiver also needs to focus until he has the ball in his hands. Many dropped passes happen when receivers try to take off running before they have fully caught the ball.

Running

Every player on the field might carry the ball at some point. But it is usually the job of a running back. A good ballcarrier has to hold on to the ball. Defenders try to force fumbles when they make tackles. So the runner needs a tight grip. He wraps his fingers around the front end of the ball. Then he tucks the other point into his elbow. He also tries to hold the ball tight to his body. Runners also wrap up the ball with their other arm when they are about to be tackled.

Leonard Fournette of the Tampa Bay Buccaneers keeps his eyes up the field as he grips the ball on a running play.

Running backs often carry the ball. These players need to see the field well. They know where defenders are coming from. They also need to be patient and let their linemen make blocks to create open running lanes.

Pass Defense

On running plays, all defensive players have the same job. They want to tackle the ballcarrier as soon as possible. But on passing plays, a defender can either rush the quarterback or cover a receiver.

Defensive linemen often rush the quarterback. But they have to get past the offensive linemen first. They do this by overpowering an offensive lineman or quickly going around him.

Linebackers and defensive backs can rush the quarterback too. This is called a blitz. However, on most plays they cover receivers. To do that, they need speed and quickness. It's also helpful to be able to catch the ball. Any pass can be intercepted. So defensive backs need good hands.

Kicking and Punting

Most teams have one kicker and one punter. Kickers, holders, and long snappers form a unit. They work together to practice the snap, placement, and kick on field goals and extra points. It takes perfect timing to do it right.

The best punters have good footwork. They also drop the ball toward their foot the same way. Laces should be up and the nose of the ball pointing down. To get the most distance, a punter swings his leg all the way through the kicking motion. That gives punts more power. When he is done, his kicking foot should be above his head.

Mental Skills

The best football players master both the physical and the mental side of football. Every football team has a playbook. Players must study it in order to know their jobs on every play. This helps the team succeed.

Players can also study their opponents by watching films of another team's games. That will

Every football position has a job on every play.

help a team figure out patterns in how another team plays. Players who know what the other team is trying to do have an advantage.

Finally, players must control their emotions. In a physical sport, a player who loses his temper can hurt his team. He can be called for penalties. But he can also get distracted and forget his job. Either way, he hurts the team by not staying focused.

Quarterback

The quarterback is usually the focus of the offense. Before the play, he tells his offense what to do. He also helps everyone line up in the right place.

During a play, the quarterback can hand off, pass, or run with the ball. On passing plays, the quarterback must keep his eyes downfield and look for open receivers. This has to happen fast. A slow quarterback will be pressured by the defense. He might not be able to pass the ball.

At youth levels, many quarterbacks run as much as they pass. For many years, professional

Lamar Jackson

Lamar Jackson is a good running quarterback. In 2019, Jackson led the NFL with 36 touchdown passes while playing for the Baltimore Ravens. He also ran for more than 1,200 yards. He was the second quarterback ever to run for 1,000 yards in a single season.

quarterbacks ran only if they had to. But now many top-level quarterbacks are good runners too.

Christian McCaffrey (23) of the San Francisco 49ers bursts through a hole.

Running Back

A running back takes a handoff from the quarterback. Then he looks for open space to run. He wants to gain as many yards as possible.

There are two main types of running backs. Halfbacks mostly run with the ball or catch passes. Fullbacks usually block for the halfback.

Sometimes the fullback gets to carry the ball. Many fullbacks are also used as receivers.

Running backs can be many different sizes. Christian McCaffrey of the San Francisco 49ers is 5 feet, 11 inches tall, 205 pounds, and very quick. The Tennessee Titans' Derrick Henry is 6 feet, 3 inches tall and 247 pounds. He uses his strength to run through defenders.

Derrick Henry (22) led the NFL with 2,027 rushing yards and 17 touchdowns during the 2020 season.

Wide Receiver

Wide receivers help move an offense down the field by catching passes. They are often the fastest players on the field. They typically line up outside the offensive linemen at the start of a play.

Catching the ball is an important job for receivers, of course. To get in the best position to do this, a receiver must follow a good route.

Davante Adams (17) of the Las Vegas Raiders led the NFL with 14 touchdown catches in 2022.

The quarterback knows where the receivers are supposed to go. Sometimes he throws the ball to a spot toward which the receiver is moving. That's why it's important to run the proper route.

Wide receivers also block. They usually block on running plays. A receiver blocking far down the field can help a running back on a long run.

Tampa Bay Buccaneers receiver Mike Evans makes a leaping catch in a 2022 game.

Tight End

The tight end position is a cross between a receiver and a lineman. On running plays, tight ends block defensive linemen and linebackers. On passing plays, tight ends run routes just like wide receivers. That means the tight end has to be big, fast, strong, and quick.

The tight end lines up next

Tight end Travis Kelce of the Kansas City Chiefs hauls in a pass.

Chicago Bears tight end Cole Kmet, *center*, blocks for quarterback Justin Fields, *right*.

to the offensive linemen. Teams with talented pass-catching tight ends will find different ways to get them the ball. Sometimes a tight end will even line up away from the line, like a wide receiver, on a passing play.

Offensive Linemen

Each team has five offensive linemen on most plays. Two tackles line up on each end. Next to them are two guards. The center lines up in the middle. The center is often the leader of the offensive line. He snaps the ball to start the play. But before the play starts, the center might call out blocking assignments for the other linemen.

The linemen's job is to block. On running plays, linemen

try to push defenders back. They can keep moving down the field to open new lanes for the running back.

On passing plays, linemen step backward. That way they can form a protective space for the quarterback. This space is called a pocket.

Eligible Receivers

On most plays, offensive linemen are not allowed to catch passes. They can do so only if they have told the referee before the play that they are lining up as a receiver. The referee then announces to both teams that the lineman is allowed to be a receiver for that play only.

Defensive Linemen

Defensive linemen are the first line of defense for the team without the ball. Usually a team has three or four defensive linemen on the field, depending on the formation. Linemen on the edges of the line are called defensive ends. Linemen who play in the middle are called defensive tackles.

The most famous defensive linemen are the ones who sack the quarterback a lot.

Defensive ends usually get the most sacks. Defensive ends are often both strong and quick.

Stopping the run is also important. Defensive linemen can tackle running backs. They also help by handling so many blockers that other players, such as linebackers, have more room to make plays. Many defensive linemen can play well without making a lot of tackles.

Linebacker

Linebackers play between the defensive linemen and the defensive backs. In a standard 4–3 defense, a team will have a middle linebacker and two outside linebackers. The linebackers can have many jobs, depending on the play.

On running plays, linebackers chase down running backs. On passing plays, linebackers might rush the quarterback. They might also drop back to cover a running back or tight end. Linebackers have to be big enough to take on blockers, but quick enough to defend passes.

A middle linebacker is often the leader of the defense. He calls out instructions before every play. And because linebackers do so much, they are often the team's leading tacklers.

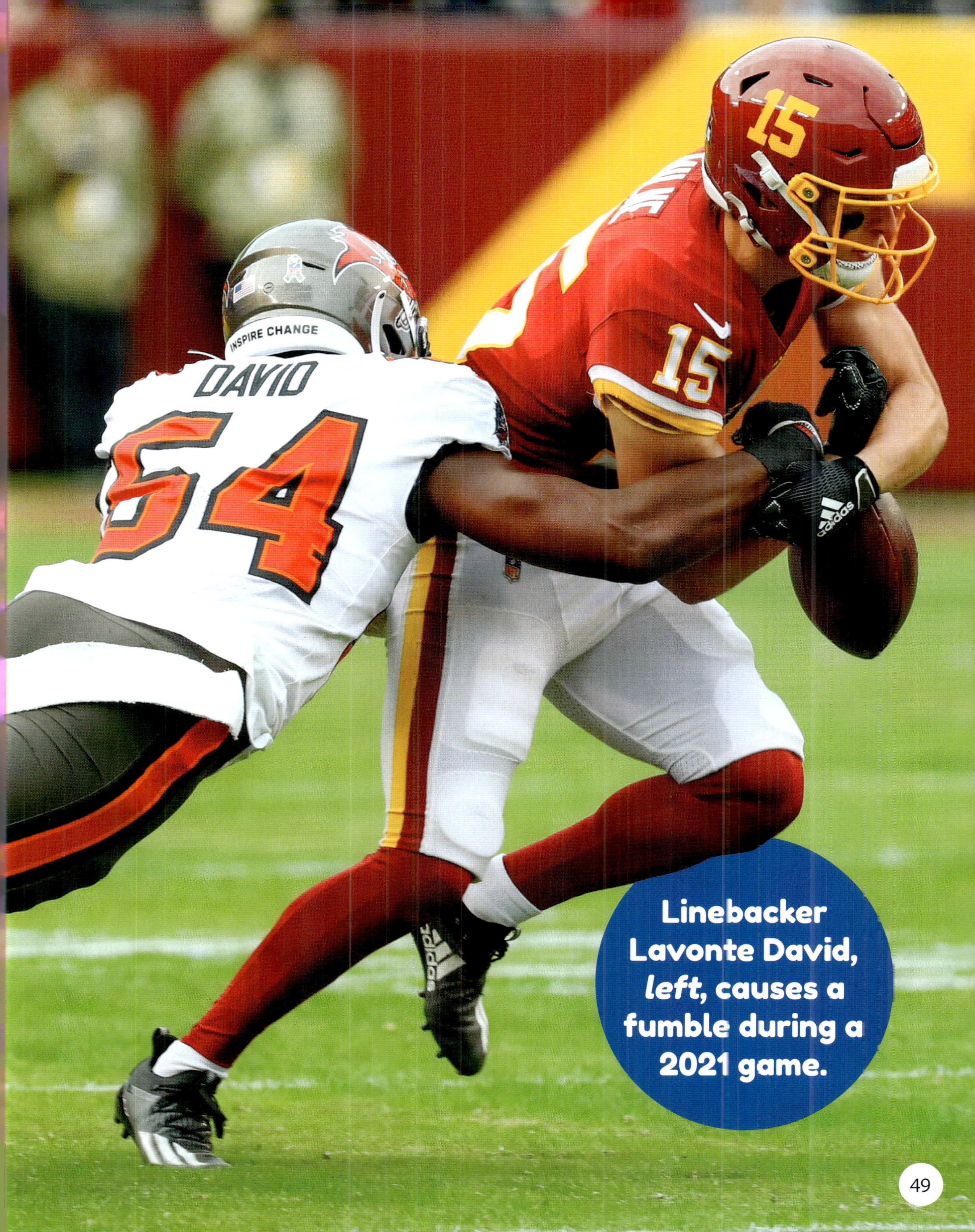

Linebacker Lavonte David, *left*, causes a fumble during a 2021 game.

Defensive Back

There are two positions in the defensive backfield. Cornerbacks line up across from wide receivers. Their main job is to cover receivers down the field on passing plays. Safeties cover the deep areas of the field and help cornerbacks defend long passes.

Cornerbacks are often smaller than the receivers they're covering. But speed and good positioning can help them cover taller

Dallas Cowboys cornerback Kelvin Joseph, *right,* knocks down a pass in a 2022 game against the Indianapolis Colts.

Cornerback Sauce Gardner of the New York Jets covers a receiver during a game on January 1, 2023.

players. They can also hit the receiver in the first five yards of his route. That can disrupt the offense's timing.

The strong safety often plays closer to the line of scrimmage. That way he can help stop a running play. He can also help cover tight ends and running backs. The free safety is deeper. He's the last line of defense on long passing plays.

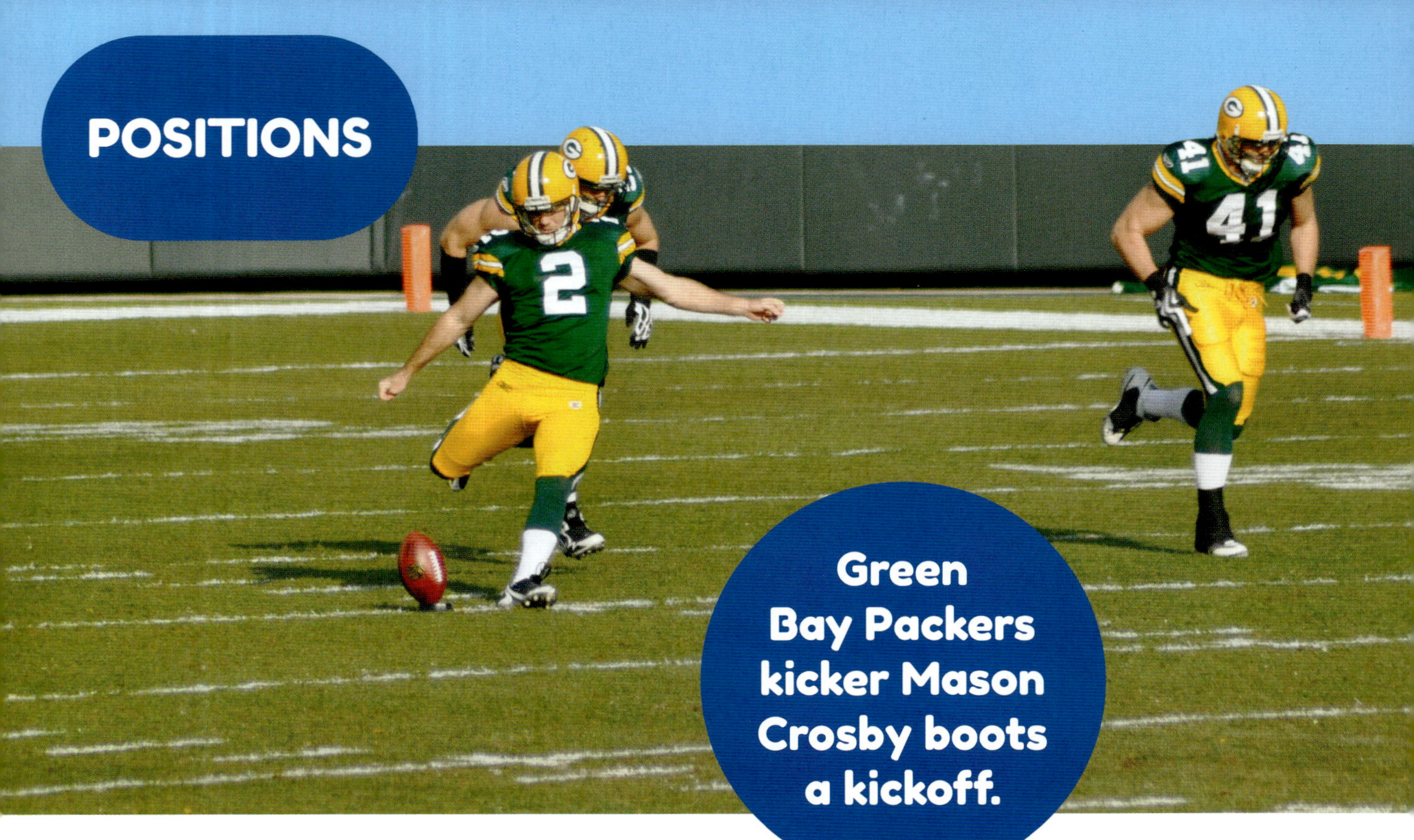

Kicker and Punter

Kickers and punters have special jobs. They focus on their kicking duties. The kicker is also sometimes called the placekicker. He kicks extra points after touchdowns as well as field goals. Most kickers also handle kickoff duties.

Sometimes the punter is in charge of kickoffs instead. But the punter's main job is to punt the ball on fourth down. He tries to give the opposing offense a bad field position from which to start its next drive. If he's close enough, a punter will try to land the ball inside the opponents' 10-yard line. He has to avoid kicking the ball into the end zone, however. Doing so is called a touchback. If this happens, the other team gets the ball at the 20-yard line.

Equipment

Football equipment has changed a lot over the years. There was a time when helmets were made of leather and didn't have face masks. Now, players wear helmets made of plastic. Helmets are designed to help protect players from concussions. The helmets have a hard shell with padding inside.

Face masks come in different designs. Players can choose which design suits them best. A mouth guard made of molded plastic protects the player's teeth.

Early football helmets did not protect players' faces.

Other parts of the body are covered with padding. Most players wear pads on their shoulders, hips, thighs, and knees. Those pads protect against injuries like bruises. Knee injuries are common in football. Some players wear knee braces to help protect themselves.

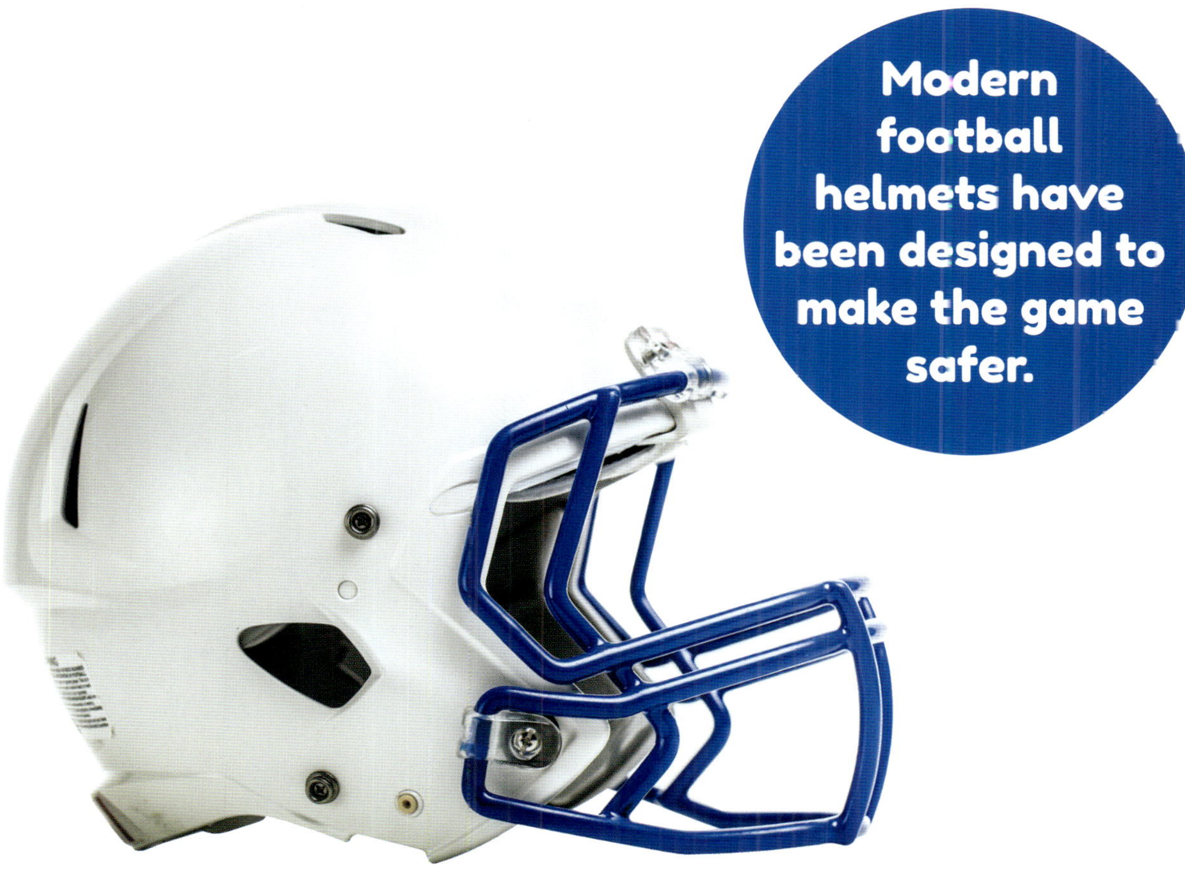

Proper Technique

One of the best ways to prevent an injury is by learning proper techniques. Many injuries happen during tackles. A player who knows the right way to tackle can avoid getting hurt.

The tackler should face the ballcarrier with his feet shoulder-width apart. He should lead with his shoulder, not his head. Most neck injuries come from tackling with the helmet first.

Once a defender has squared up, he should bend his legs and use their power to drive through the ballcarrier. The defender's helmet will move to the side of the ballcarrier's torso or legs. The shoulder should hit the runner first. Then the arms should wrap around the ballcarrier. That helps prevent injuries for both players.

Two defenders wrap their arms around a ballcarrier while making a tackle.

Popularity in America

Football has been the United States' most popular sport since the early 1970s. Millions of Americans watch football all weekend long. The NFL's Super Bowl is often the most-watched TV

Some college stadiums, like the one at Ohio State University, hold more than 100,000 fans.

event of the year in the United States.

Youth participation in football has dropped in recent years. The big reason is health concerns for young players. As a result, organizers are looking at ways to make football safer.

Around the World

In most countries, "football" is the sport the United States calls soccer. But "American football" is growing in other countries. The NFL has even played games Mexico, England, and Germany.

Football and Television

Television has helped make football very popular. The rectangular field is easy to film. That makes games easy to watch for fans at home.

Football first became popular on TV in the late 1950s. In 1970, the NFL agreed to put one game on Monday night. Fans began looking forward to Monday Night Football every week.

Now, the NFL plays games on Sunday nights and Thursday nights too. Many Sunday night games are set up to show the best teams playing each other. That makes them bigger events.

The 1958 NFL Championship

The NFL Championship Game in 1958 was one of the first big football games on TV. The Baltimore Colts beat the New York Giants 23–17 in overtime. It was broadcast to the entire country. Around 45 million fans watched it live.

Cameramen capture the action of a football game from the sidelines.

Origins of the Sport

Football began in the 1800s. The first college football game was played on November 6, 1869. It was between Princeton University and Rutgers University in New Jersey. Eastern schools like Harvard University and Yale University soon began playing their own versions of the sport. In football's early days, the game was very violent. Some players even died.

The schools started the Intercollegiate Football Association (IFA). One of its jobs was to come up with a set of rules. A man named Walter Camp led the way. Camp had played at Yale. He helped the IFA make many rules that are familiar today. That included 11 players per side and a line of scrimmage. Camp's efforts also helped football become safer for players.

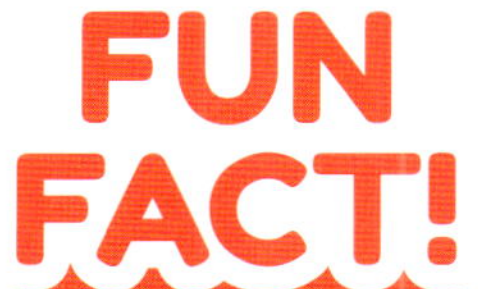

The Early NFL

In 1920, the owners of four professional football teams in Ohio met to organize a new league. Soon other teams around the Midwest joined. In 1922, the league was named the National Football League. Many of the original teams did not last.

In 1946, the Cleveland Rams moved from Ohio to Los Angeles, California. That gave the NFL its first western team. A rival league called the All-America Football Conference (AAFC) formed that same season. It lasted only four years. The NFL added three of its clubs. That brought the NFL up to 13 teams.

The AFL/NFL Merger

In 1960, another rival league started. The American Football League (AFL) had eight teams. The NFL then added more teams and had 16 by 1969.

The Super Bowl

The NFL's Green Bay Packers won the first two AFL-NFL Championship Games easily. Many people thought that showed the NFL was the better league. But the next year the AFL's New York Jets surprisingly beat the NFL's Baltimore Colts and showed the two leagues were even.

AFL games featured lots of passing. They were also high-scoring. NFL teams mostly ran the ball. Fans began to wonder if the AFL was more exciting than the NFL.

Before the 1966 season, the NFL and AFL decided to merge. They also decided to play the first AFL-NFL Championship Game. The annual game would

eventually be called the Super Bowl.

When the 1970 season started, the AFL teams were NFL members. The league now had two conferences. One was the National Football Conference (NFC). The other was the American Football Conference (AFC).

Defense Rules

The 1970s were dominated by teams with great defenses. The Pittsburgh Steelers won four Super Bowls in the decade. Their defense was called the "Steel Curtain." The 1972 Miami Dolphins became the first NFL team to finish a season undefeated. They were led by the "No-Name Defense."

The Dallas Cowboys played in five Super Bowls in the 1970s and won two. Their "Doomsday Defense" led the way. The Minnesota Vikings won three NFC titles behind their great defensive line. It was called the "Purple People Eaters."

By the end of the decade, the NFL changed some rules to help offenses. Defensive backs could no longer push receivers all the way down the field. And an offensive lineman could now extend his arms when pass blocking. It set up a new era of offense.

Defensive tackle Bob Lilly was a star for the Cowboys' Doomsday Defense in the 1970s.

The Rise of Offense

The 1980s and 1990s had several legendary quarterbacks. Joe Montana led the San Francisco 49ers to four Super Bowl victories. John Elway brought the Denver Broncos to five Super Bowls with his strong arm. He won two championships. Miami Dolphins quarterback Dan Marino broke many NFL passing records.

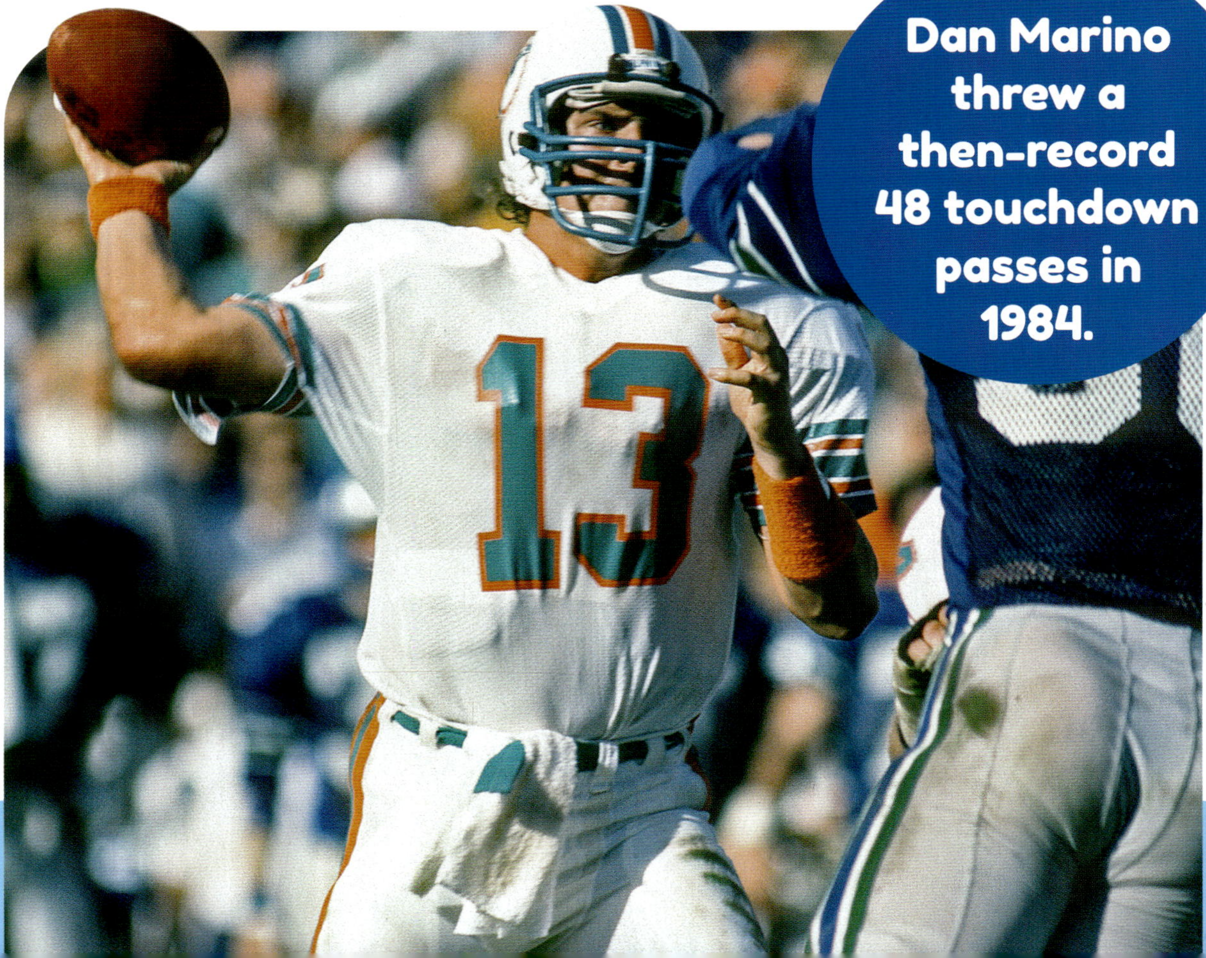

Dan Marino threw a then-record 48 touchdown passes in 1984.

Jim Kelly quarterbacked the Buffalo Bills to four straight Super Bowls in the early 1990s. But Buffalo lost all four. They lost to the Dallas Cowboys twice. Dallas was the decade's best team. Its offensive trio of quarterback Troy Aikman, running back Emmitt Smith, and wide receiver Michael Irvin was tough to stop. The Cowboys won three Super Bowls in the 1990s.

John Elway holds up the Vince Lombardi Trophy after winning Super Bowl XXXII in January 1998.

Modern Legends

Peyton Manning began playing for the Indianapolis Colts in 1998. Tom Brady first played for the New England Patriots in 2000. The two quarterbacks dominated the next several years. Manning often had the better statistics. But no quarterback in NFL history has won as many

Peyton Manning, *left*, and Tom Brady had a fierce rivalry in the 2000s.

Super Bowls as Brady. He eventually moved to the Tampa Bay Buccaneers. Brady won his seventh Super Bowl there after the 2020 season.

Continued rule changes helped more quarterbacks thrive. Aaron Rodgers of the Green Bay Packers and Drew Brees of the New Orleans Saints climbed the all-time leaderboards. Then, in the late 2010s, Patrick Mahomes joined the Kansas City Chiefs. His strong passing arm led that team to Super Bowl wins after the 2019 and 2022 seasons.

Youth Football

Children can play football starting at age five. Most play in leagues like Pop Warner. They play kids in their own age-group. But players are also separated by weight. This is done to keep youth football safe for all players.

Many communities offer touch and flag football options for young players. NFL FLAG is the league's official flag

More than 300,000 kids play Pop Warner football every year.

football organization. It sets up leagues for players from ages five to 17. More than 500,000 young athletes play NFL FLAG every season. Cities may have leagues through local organizations too.

High School Football

High school football is a popular tradition in many communities. Fans pack local stadiums every Friday night. In many states, the high school championship games are played in NFL or college stadiums. They are also on TV. High school football is particularly popular in Texas. Some high schools in the state draw crowds of more than 10,000 fans.

A receiver catches a pass during a high school football game in Texas.

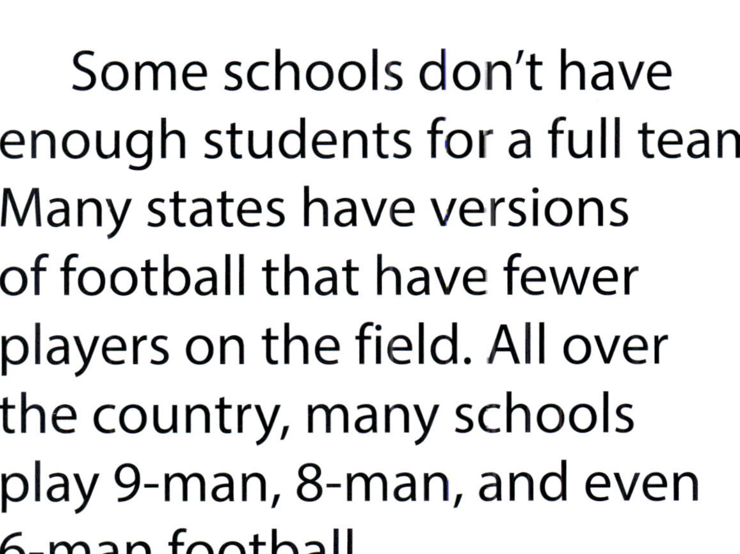

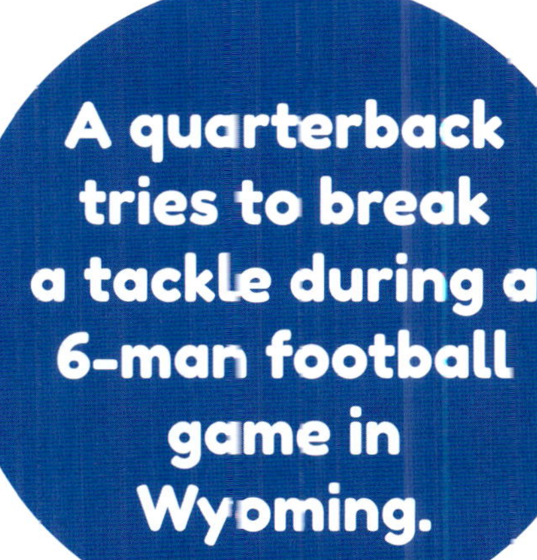

Some schools don't have enough students for a full team. Many states have versions of football that have fewer players on the field. All over the country, many schools play 9-man, 8-man, and even 6-man football.

A quarterback tries to break a tackle during a 6-man football game in Wyoming.

College Football

The first US football players were college students. And college football is still popular. Hundreds of colleges from all over the country play football every fall. The biggest schools play at the Football Bowl Subdivision (FBS) level. There are also many other levels for smaller schools.

Rivalries are a big part of college football. Schools often face opponents from nearby. Sometimes teams have been playing each other for years. Those traditions help make college

University of Alabama quarterback Tua Tagovailoa makes a pass in a 2018 game.

football special. Another tradition is one where teams play in special bowl games at the end of the year.

College football now has a playoff to decide a national champion. It wasn't always that way. Coaches and sportswriters used to vote on the champion after the bowl games were over. The playoff system started in 2014.

The NFL

The NFL regular season begins in September. It ends in early January. The league has 32 teams. They are split into two conferences. One is the AFC. The other is the NFC. Each conference has four smaller groups of four teams each. These are called divisions. Each team plays 17 games in a season. At the end of the year, the winners of every division make the playoffs. Three other teams in each conference get wild card spots in the playoffs.

The playoffs have four rounds. For the first three, teams play against other conference opponents. Once each conference has only one team left, those teams meet in the Super Bowl. The Super Bowl winner is the league champion.

Map of NFL Teams

The Super Bowl

The Super Bowl is the biggest football game of the year. It takes place in February. Millions of fans watch it on TV around the world. It has become much more than just a game. Every year, the most popular entertainers in the world perform the halftime show. Companies also pay millions of dollars to run commercials

The Blue Angels fly over Super Bowl 50 on February 7, 2016, in Santa Clara, California.

during game breaks. Some people watch just to see the advertisements.

The first game to be called the Super Bowl was actually Super Bowl III, held in January 1969. The name was suggested by Kansas City Chiefs owner Lamar Hunt. He said it came from his children playing with a toy called a Super Ball.

Stadiums

NFL stadiums are among the most expensive and high-tech buildings in the United States. In Arlington, Texas, AT&T Stadium opened in 2009. It cost $1.2 billion to build. The highlight is a 25,000-square-foot (2,323 square meter) video board that hangs over the field. The stadium holds 80,000 fans for football games. That can expand to 100,000 for concerts and other events.

The Atlanta Falcons play in Mercedes-Benz Stadium. It opened in 2017. The glass walls and roof allow natural light into the building. The roof can also be opened when the weather is nice.

AT&T Stadium in Arlington, Texas, once held 105,121 fans for a game between the Dallas Cowboys and the New York Giants.

Dallas Cowboys

The Dallas Cowboys joined the NFL in 1960. In 1966, they started a streak of 20 straight winning seasons. During that stretch they won 13 division titles, five NFC championships, and two Super Bowls. In 1978, a league video called the Cowboys "America's Team." The nickname stuck.

Those Cowboys were led by head coach Tom Landry. He held that title from the team's birth through 1988. Landry's teams were fierce on defense. They also had offensive stars like quarterback Roger Staubach and running back Tony Dorsett. The next Cowboys dynasty emerged in the early 1990s. Dallas won three Super Bowls in four years.

FUN FACT!

The Dallas Cowboys are one of two teams that play a game every Thanksgiving. The Detroit Lions are the other.

Quarterback Troy Aikman, *right*, and running back Emmitt Smith won three Super Bowls together in the 1990s.

Green Bay Packers

The Green Bay Packers are one of the oldest NFL teams. They were formed in 1919 and joined the NFL two years later. The team won nine NFL championships in the pre-Super Bowl era. Most of those came under team founder Curly Lambeau. Today the Packers play at Lambeau Field in Green Bay, Wisconsin. They won the first two Super

Lambeau Field has been the Packers' home stadium since 1957.

Bowls behind legendary coach Vince Lombardi. The Super Bowl winners are now given the Vince Lombardi Trophy.

The Packers won Super Bowl XXXI after the 1996 season. The team's star that year was quarterback Brett Favre. His replacement, Aaron Rodgers, won Super Bowl XLV after the 2010 season.

New England Patriots

The Boston Patriots were founding members of the AFL. They began playing in 1960. In 1964, they played for the league championship. They changed their name to the New England Patriots in 1971. For the rest of the 1900s they were mostly a losing team. The highlights were two Super Bowl losses.

Everything changed in 2001. Coach Bill Belichick teamed up with quarterback Tom Brady. That year the Patriots won the Super Bowl. Soon they were a dynasty. New England won two of the next three Super Bowls, then added three more between the 2014 and 2018 seasons. Their championship wins were usually great games. They won two Super Bowls on late field goals. Their Super Bowl LI win came in overtime after falling behind 28–3.

Patriots running back James White, *center*, scores the winning touchdown in overtime in Super Bowl LI on February 5, 2017.

Pittsburgh Steelers

The Pittsburgh Steelers were founded in 1933. They made the playoffs just once in their first 37 seasons. In two seasons during World War II (1939–1945) they had to merge with other teams just to have enough players.

Head coach Chuck Noll arrived in 1969. Over the next five years, the Steelers drafted nine future Hall of Fame players. Stars like

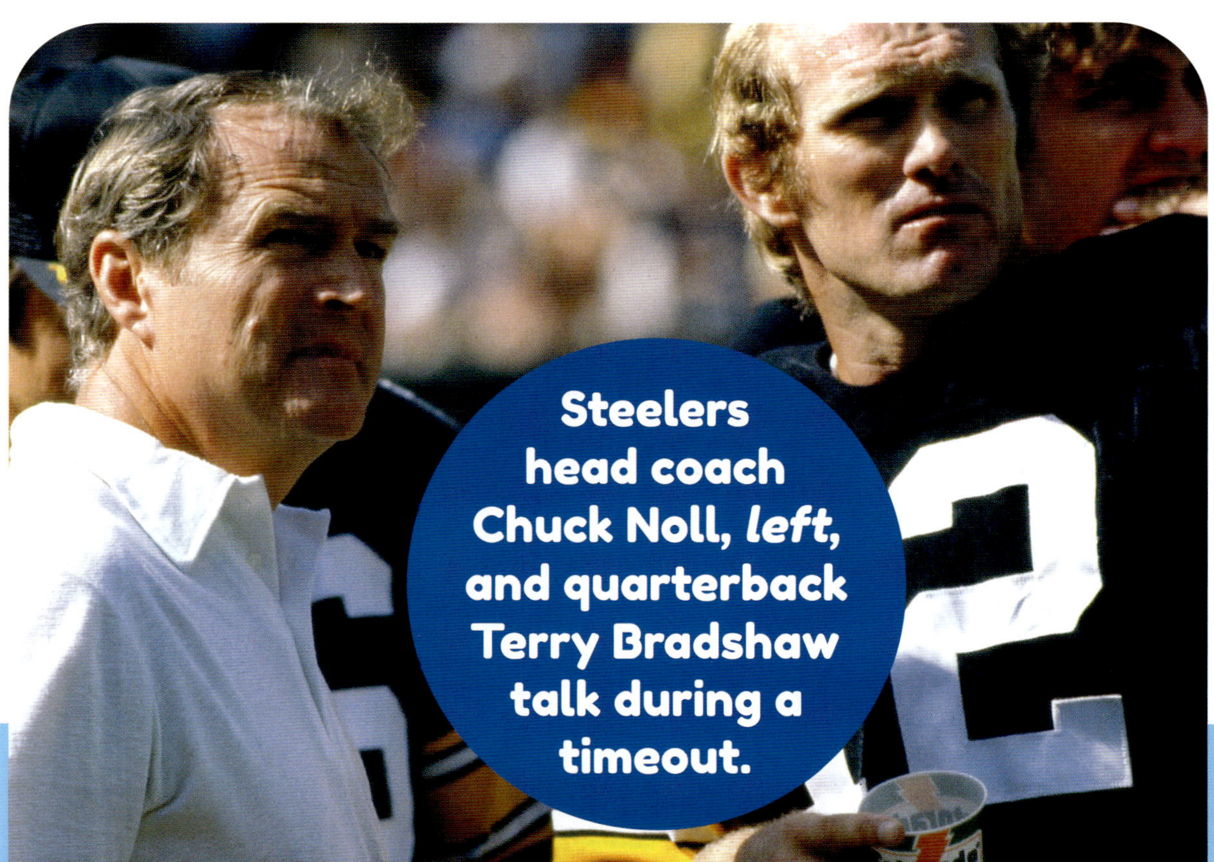

quarterback Terry Bradshaw and cornerback Mel Blount helped the Steelers win four Super Bowls between the 1974 and 1979 seasons.

Quarterback Ben Roethlisberger led the Steelers to Super Bowl wins after the 2005 and 2008 seasons. That made them the first team to win six Lombardi Trophies.

FUN FACT!

The Steelers combined their team with the Philadelphia Eagles for the 1943 season. The team was nicknamed the "Steagles."

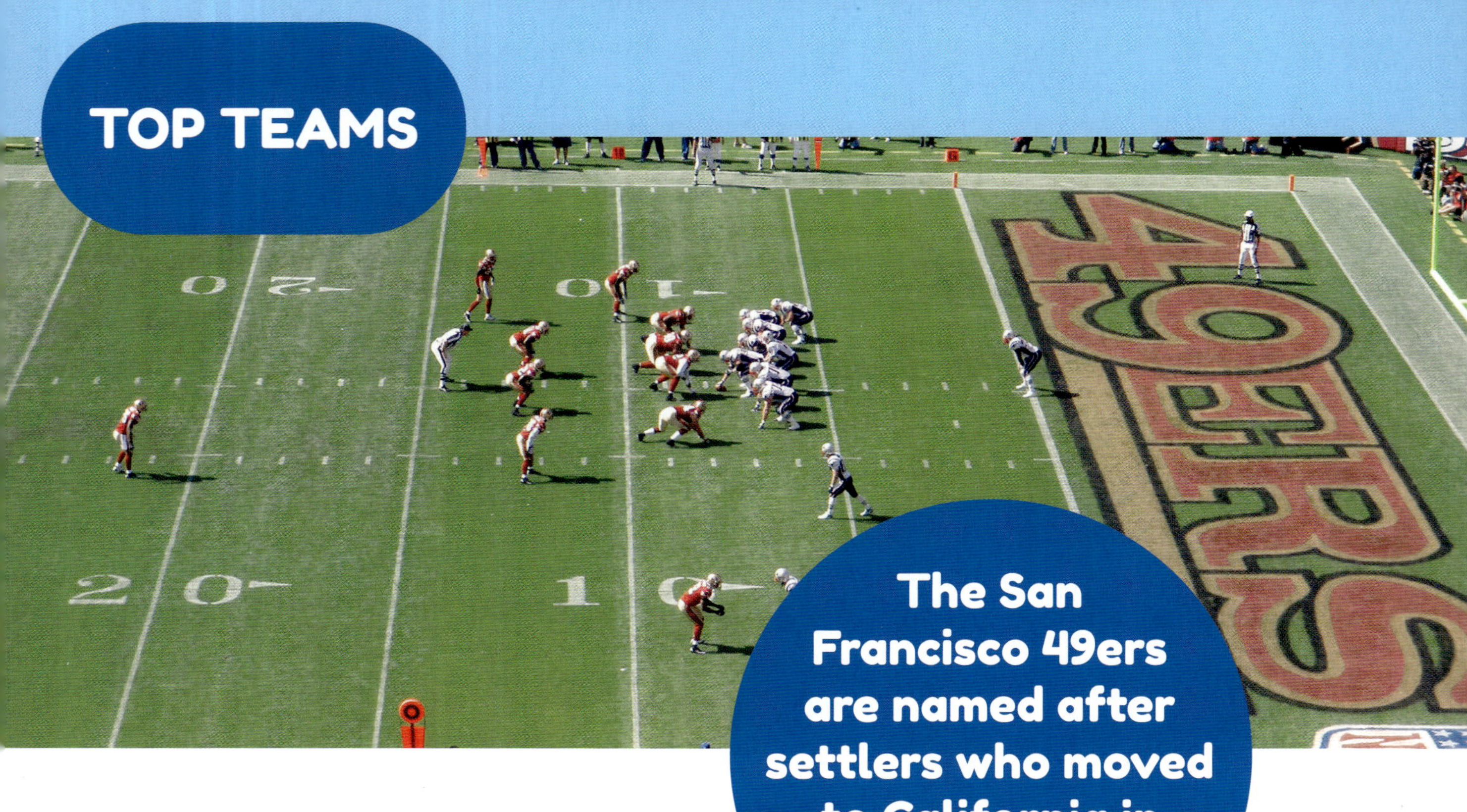

San Francisco 49ers

The San Francisco 49ers are named after settlers who moved to California in 1849 looking for gold.

The San Francisco 49ers joined the NFL in 1950 after four years in the AAFC. They reached the postseason just once in their first 20 NFL seasons. By 1980 they still had not played in a Super Bowl.

Then head coach Bill Walsh built an offense around quarterback Joe Montana throwing short passes. It became known as the "West Coast

Offense," and it was a big success. The 49ers won the Super Bowl after the 1981 and 1984 seasons.

The offense then added Hall of Fame receiver Jerry Rice. He teamed with Montana to win two more Super Bowls. Steve Young took over at quarterback and the Niners picked up a fifth title after the 1994 season. At the time, that was the most in NFL history.

Steve Young, *center*, celebrates with Jerry Rice, *left*, after the 49ers won Super Bowl XXIX on January 29, 1995.

Johnny Unitas

Johnny Unitas was known for his comeback victories. His most famous came in the 1958 NFL Championship Game. "Johnny U" led the Colts on a last-minute drive for a game-tying field goal. Then he led the winning drive in overtime.

Johnny Unitas led the NFL in touchdown passes every year from 1957 to 1960.

Joe Montana

Joe Montana earned the nickname "Joe Cool" for his steady play late in games. Montana led his teams to 31 comeback victories in the fourth quarter. His masterpiece came in Super Bowl XXIII after the 1988 season. He marched the 49ers 92 yards in less than three minutes. He then threw a game-winning touchdown pass to receiver John Taylor.

Joe Montana was named most valuable player (MVP) of the Super Bowl three times.

John Elway

Quarterback John Elway led the Denver Broncos to five Super Bowls. He lost the first three in the late 1980s and early 1990s. It took him until January 1998 to get back to the big game. That year, Elway and the Broncos beat the Green Bay Packers 31–24. Elway won again the next year before retiring with more than 51,000 passing yards and 300 touchdowns.

John Elway won his first Super Bowl at age 37.

Peyton Manning

Peyton Manning's father, Archie, spent 13 years as an NFL quarterback. His brother Eli played 16 seasons and won two Super Bowls. But Peyton was the best of them all. He picked apart defenses with his accurate passing. He won five NFL MVP Awards and led both the Indianapolis Colts and the Broncos to Super Bowl titles before retiring in 2015.

Tom Brady

Tom Brady's seven Super Bowl rings are the most of any player. He won six with the New England Patriots and one with the Tampa Bay Buccaneers. He was also Super Bowl MVP five times. Along the way, he set NFL records for career passing yards and touchdown passes.

Tom Brady retired with 89,214 passing yards.

Patrick Mahomes

Patrick Mahomes often throws tricky sidearm or no-look passes. In his second NFL season, Mahomes led the league with 50 touchdown passes and took the Kansas City Chiefs to the AFC title game. The next season, in 2019, he led the Chiefs to their first Super Bowl win in 50 years. He won another Super Bowl after the 2022 season.

Patrick Mahomes won his first NFL MVP Award in 2018.

Jim Brown

Jim Brown played only nine NFL seasons, from 1957 to 1965. In that time he won eight league rushing titles and three MVP Awards. Brown could outrun defenders with his blazing speed or run them over with his strength. The Cleveland Browns legend helped the team win the NFL title in 1964.

Walter Payton

Walter Payton was nicknamed "Sweetness." Payton was fast, quick, and powerful. He would go around, through, or even over a defense to reach the end zone. Payton also was an excellent receiver and blocker. He even threw eight touchdown passes in his career. When he retired in 1987, his 16,726 rushing yards were the all-time record.

The NFL's Man of the Year Award is named after Walter Payton.

Barry Sanders

Barry Sanders might have been the hardest running back to tackle in NFL history. The Detroit Lions star used his remarkable quickness to dart in and out of tough spots for ten seasons before retiring in 1998. During the 1997 season, he became just the third running back ever to rush for 2,000 yards in a season. It was the fourth time he led the league in rushing.

Barry Sanders runs away from three defenders in a 1998 game.

Emmitt Smith

When Sanders wasn't winning rushing titles, Emmitt Smith was. Smith won four rushing crowns in his first six NFL seasons. He also helped the Dallas Cowboys win three Super Bowls in that span. Smith became the league record holder with 164 career rushing touchdowns and 18,355 rushing yards.

Emmitt Smith ran for more than 100 yards in both Super Bowl XXVII and Super Bowl XXVIII.

Don Hutson

Don Hutson played from 1935 to 1945. At the time, most teams didn't pass much. But Hutson still caught 488 career passes. He retired with 99 touchdown catches. That record stood for 44 years. Hutson also invented many of the pass patterns that receivers still run today. Hutson was also a great safety on defense. He retired with 30 interceptions.

Jerry Rice

In 1992, Jerry Rice broke the all-time receiving touchdowns record. He was only in his eighth NFL season. Rice then played 12 more NFL seasons with the San Francisco 49ers, Oakland Raiders, and Seattle Seahawks. He retired with 197 career scores. Rice also broke NFL records for catches and total receiving yards.

FUN FACT!

Jerry Rice wasn't just good in the regular season. He played in the Super Bowl four times and scored eight touchdowns in those games.

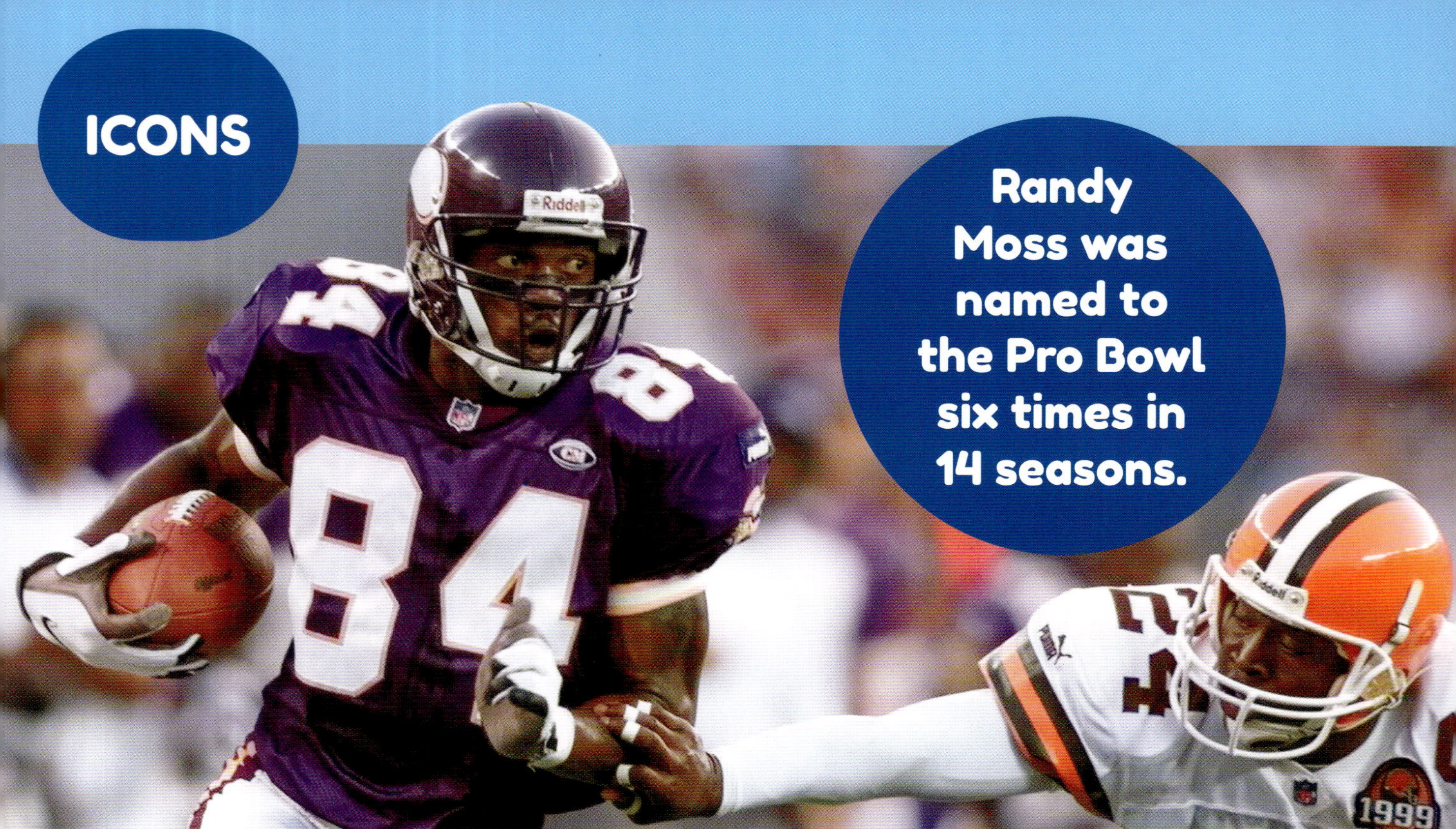

Randy Moss

Randy Moss's speed and leaping ability helped him come down with passes most receivers wouldn't touch. Moss led the NFL in touchdown catches five times. That includes a record-setting 23 in 2007. He also topped

FUN FACT!

When Larry Fitzgerald was growing up in Minnesota, he was a sideline ball boy for the Vikings. He used to get tips from Minnesota receivers, including Randy Moss.

1,000 yards in ten different seasons with the Minnesota Vikings, Oakland Raiders, and New England Patriots.

Larry Fitzgerald

Larry Fitzgerald's size and strength made him tough to defend. But his great hands made him a superstar. Most NFL receivers drop between five and ten passes in a season. Fitzgerald played for 17 years with the Arizona Cardinals. In that time he dropped only 29 passes total. When he retired in 2020, Fitzgerald was second in total catches and touchdowns. Only Jerry Rice had more.

Tony Gonzalez

Tony Gonzalez played football and basketball at the University of California. Skills from both sports helped him become a great tight end for 17 years with the Kansas City Chiefs and Atlanta Falcons. Gonzalez caught more passes for more yards and more touchdowns than any other tight end in NFL history. In 2004, his 102 receptions led the league. Only two other tight ends had ever done that.

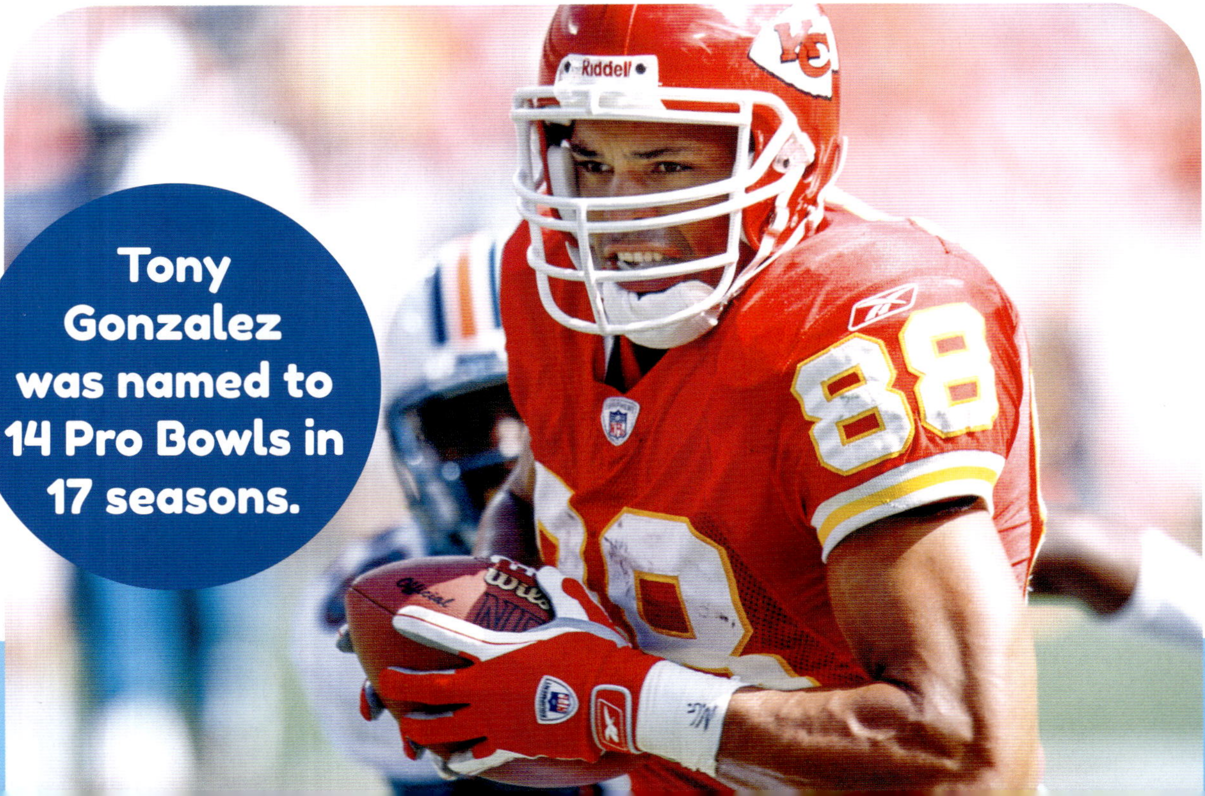

Tony Gonzalez was named to 14 Pro Bowls in 17 seasons.

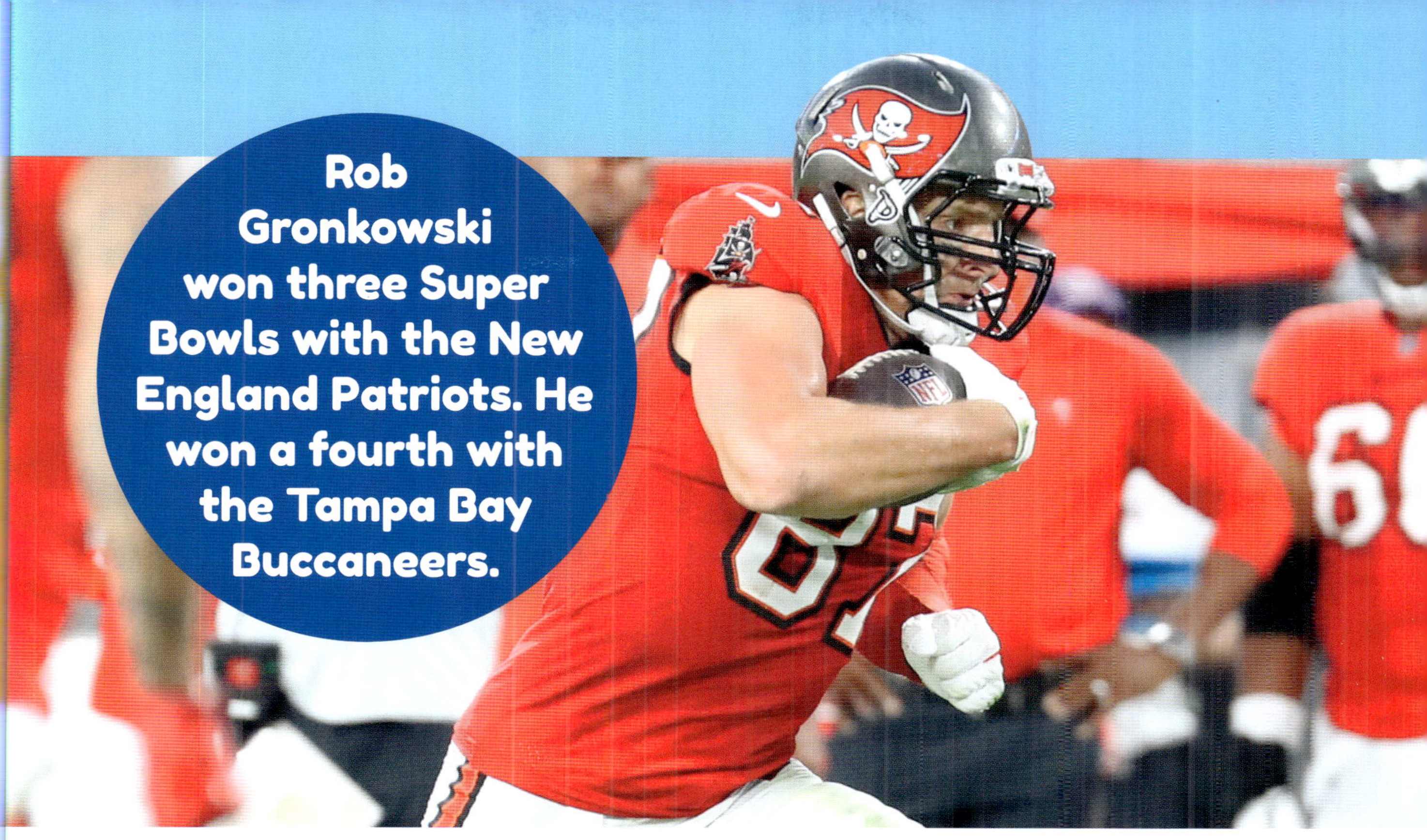

Rob Gronkowski

Rob Gronkowski was a character on and off the field with the New England Patriots and Tampa Bay Buccaneers. "Gronk" used his big frame to run over defenders. His fun-loving personality showed up in his big spikes after scoring touchdowns. He had plenty of chances to celebrate. Gronkowski retired with 92 career touchdown catches. That included a league-high 17 in 2011.

Gene Upshaw

Gene Upshaw was a big man. But his speed and quickness helped him quickly move all over the field to block for Oakland Raiders running backs. The guard was also very tough. He didn't miss a game until 1981, the final season of his 15-year career. He played in three Super Bowls, winning two. He was also the Raiders' captain for eight years.

Gene Upshaw spent his entire career with the Oakland Raiders.

Anthony Muñoz

Anthony Muñoz was voted first-team Al-Pro in nine of his 13 seasons with the Cincinnati Bengals. He overcame knee injuries in college to become one of the game's best left tackles. Muñoz was quick, strong, and mobile. He missed just three NFL games due to injuries. His leadership and blocking helped the Bengals reach two Super Bowls.

Joe Greene

"Mean" Joe Greene was the anchor of Pittsburgh's "Steel Curtain" defense that dominated the NFL in the 1970s. The defensive tackle used his strength and speed to overpower offensive linemen. Greene stopped opponents' running backs and also was a great pass rusher. He was voted to ten Pro Bowls in 13 seasons.

Joe Greene was named the NFL's Defensive Player of the Year twice.

Bruce Smith (78) sacks New York Giants quarterback Dave Brown during a game in 1996.

Bruce Smith

Bruce Smith chased down quarterbacks for nearly 20 years. The defensive end is the NFL's all-time sacks leader with 200 quarterback takedowns. Smith often faced the offense's best lineman. Few ever gave him trouble. Smith had 13 seasons with at least ten sacks. He was named NFL Defensive Player of the Year twice and helped the Buffalo Bills reach four Super Bowls.

Dick Butkus

Chicago Bears linebacker Dick Butkus was one of the league's toughest players ever. Strong, fast, tough, and driven, Butkus was quick enough to cover backs and tight ends. He also punished any opposing ballcarrier who came his way.

A knee injury cut his career short in 1973. But the eight-time Pro Bowler left a lasting mark on the linebacker position.

Dick Butkus had 22 interceptions and recovered 27 fumbles in his career.

Lawrence Taylor, *left*, pressures Chicago Bears quarterback Jim McMahon during a playoff game in January 1986.

Lawrence Taylor

Before Lawrence Taylor came around in 1981, linebackers didn't rush quarterbacks much. He used his speed to blow past offensive linemen. Taylor was also strong enough to go through them. He led the NFL with 20.5 sacks in 1986. That year Taylor was named league MVP. He also helped the New York Giants win their first Super Bowl.

Ronnie Lott

Ronnie Lott played cornerback early in his career. He picked off seven passes and returned three for touchdowns as a rookie in 1981. That season, he helped the San Francisco 49ers win their first of four Super Bowls in the 1980s. Lott eventually moved to free safety. There he became known for his big hits until his retirement in 1994.

Deion Sanders

Deion Sanders could change a game in many ways. He shut down opposing receivers over

Ronnie Lott returns an interception during a playoff game in 1984.

14 seasons with five teams. He also returned six punts and three kickoffs for touchdowns. "Prime Time" was so feared that quarterbacks rarely threw in his direction. Sanders had 53 career interceptions. He returned nine of them for touchdowns.

Ray Guy

Ray Guy was the first punter to be chosen with a first-round draft pick. He quickly showed why the Oakland Raiders wanted him so badly. Guy boomed his punts so high that his teammates were able to close in on the returner before he caught the ball. Guy also handled the Raiders' kickoff duties. He was a seven-time Pro Bowler and three-time first-team All-Pro pick.

Adam Vinatieri

Adam Vinatieri delivered clutch kicks many times in his career for the New England Patriots and the Indianapolis Colts. He won Super Bowl XXXVI on a 48-yarder as time ran out. Two seasons later, he kicked another late winner for the Patriots in the Super Bowl. Vinatieri played until 2019. He retired having scored more points than any other NFL player.

Adam Vinatieri celebrates after kicking the winning field goal in Super Bowl XXXVI on February 3, 2002.

Paul Brown

Paul Brown changed how coaches do their jobs. He introduced film study and playbooks. Brown helped start two teams. The Cleveland Browns were named after him. He won four AAFC titles and three NFL championships there before leaving in 1962. Brown then helped start the Cincinnati Bengals, coaching the team from 1968 to 1975.

Coach Paul Brown gives instructions to Cleveland Browns quarterback Frank Ryan during a game in 1962.

Vince Lombardi

In 1959, Vince Lombardi became the Green Bay Packers coach. The season before, the Packers had finished 1-10-1. Lombardi improved them to 7–5. Within two seasons they won the NFL title. It was the start of five NFL titles in seven years. The final two also included wins in what is now called the Super Bowl. Lombardi was a tough, disciplined leader. But he also cared greatly for his players. And they were fiercely loyal to him.

Don Shula coached the Miami Dolphins to a perfect 17–0 season in 1972.

Don Shula

Don Shula coached the Baltimore Colts and Miami Dolphins from 1963 to 1995. In that time he had only two losing seasons. Shula won a record 328 games. In the 1970s he featured a heavy run game. The Dolphins used that to win two Super Bowls. In the 1980s, he built a record-setting passing attack around strong-armed quarterback Dan Marino. In all, Shula won 16 division titles and reached the Super Bowl six times.

Bill Belichick

Bill Belichick lost more games than he won in his first head coaching job with the Cleveland Browns. But when he took over the New England Patriots in 2000, Belichick became a legend. He led New England to ten wins or more for 17 straight years. He also took the Patriots to nine Super Bowls in his first 19 years. That was more than any other coach. New England went 6–3 in those championship games.

Bill Belichick reached the playoffs in 16 of his first 19 seasons with the New England Patriots.

GLOSSARY

All-Pro
An award given out at the end of each NFL season to the best players at each position.

artificial turf
A substance used on sports fields to simulate real grass.

blitz
When a linebacker or defensive back attacks the line of scrimmage to stop a run or sack the quarterback.

clutch
An important or pressure-packed situation.

dynasty
A team that has an extended period of success, usually winning multiple championships in the process.

fumble
Losing the ball and allowing an opponent the chance to recover it.

goal line
The edge of the end zone a player must cross with the ball to score a touchdown.

interception
A pass intended for an offensive player that is caught by a defensive player.

line of scrimmage
The place on the field where a play starts.

rookie
A professional athlete in his or her first year of competition.

sack
A tackle of the quarterback behind the line of scrimmage before he can pass the ball.

More Books to Read

Graves, Will. *GOATs of Football*. Abdo, 2022.

Hansen, Grace. *Tom Brady: NFL Great and Super Bowl MVP*. Abdo, 2022.

Wilner, Barry. *Great Football Debates*. Abdo, 2019.

Online Resources

To learn more about football, please visit **abdobooklinks.com** or scan this QR code. These links are routinely monitored and updated to provide the most current information available.

INDEX

Cover Photos: Amy Myers/Shutterstock Images, front (left); Nic Antaya/Getty Images Sport/Getty Images, front (center); Joe SA Photos/Shutterstock Images, front (right); Benoit Daoust/Shutterstock Images, front (background); Jayne Kamin-Oncea/Getty Images Sport/Getty Images, back

Interior Photos: Steve Jacobson/Shutterstock Images, 1, 7, 16, 28, 29, 49, 109, 111; iStockphoto, 3, 18, 19, 57; Susan Leggett/Shutterstock Images, 4; Joe SA Photos/Shutterstock Images, 5, 21, 26, 27, 44, 75; MPH Photos/Shutterstock Images, 8; James D. Smith/AP Images, 9; Pavlo Kovalov/iStockphoto, 11; Shutterstock Images, 12, 40, 54, 59; Nic Antaya/Getty Images Sport/Getty Images, 13; Richard Paul Kane/Shutterstock Images, 14, 33; Keith Johnston/Shutterstock Images, 15; Soule' Photography/Shutterstock Images, 17, 24; YES Market Media/Shutterstock Images, 22; Woodys Photos/Shutterstock Images, 23; Gavin Napier/Shutterstock Images, 25; Ryan Kang/AP Images, 30; Tony Tomsic/AP Images, 31, 67, 82, 92, 105, 116, 117, 122, 123; Ruth Peterkin/Shutterstock Images, 32; Phase4 Studios/Shutterstock Images, 34; Peter Read Miller/AP Images, 35, 103, 107; Jack Dempsey/AP Images, 37; Terrell Lloyd/AP Images, 38; Phelan M. Ebenhack/AP Images, 39; Greg Trott/AP Images, 41; David Eulitt/Getty Images Sport/Getty Images, 42; Duane Burleson/AP Images, 43; Cooper Neill/AP Images, 45; John J. Klaiber Jr./Shutterstock Images, 46; G. Newman Lowrance/AP Images, 47, 110; Jeffrey Brown/Icon Sportswire/Getty Images, 50; Jeff Lewis/AP Images, 51; Mark Herreid/Shutterstock Images, 52; Andy Lewis/Icon Sportswire/Getty Images, 53; Marilyn Nieves/iStockphoto, 55; Jamie Lamor Thompson/Shutterstock Images, 58, 78; Brett Carlsen/Getty Images Sport/Getty Images, 61; Oscar White/Corbis Historical/VCG/Getty Images, 62; Images of Yale individuals (RU 684)/Manuscripts and Archives/Yale University Library, 63; Bettmann/Getty Images, 64, 106; Focus on Sport/Getty Images, 65, 69, 102, 120, 124; Al Messerschmidt/AP Images, 68; George Gojkovich/Getty Images Sport/Getty Images, 70; Doug Collier/AFP/Getty Images, 71; Jim Rogash/Getty Images Sport/Getty Images, 72; Focus on Sport/Getty Images Sport/Getty Images, 73, 96; Peter Weber/Shutterstock Images, 74; Prentice C. James/Cal Sport Media/ZUMA Wire/AP Images, 76; Andy Carpenean/Laramie Boomerang/AP Images, 77; Justin Casterline/Getty Images Sport/Getty Images, 79; ABDO Publishing, 81; Spc. Brandon C. Dyer/US Department of Defense, 83; Ken Durden/Shutterstock Images, 84–85; Focus on Sport/Getty Images, 87; Brian Bahr/Allsport/Getty Images Sport/Getty Images, 88; James Brey/iStockphoto, 89; Joseph Sohm/Shutterstock Images, 90; Charlie Riedel/AP Images, 91; Chuck Burton/AP Images, 93; Eric Broder Van Dyke/Shutterstock Images, 94; Eric Risberg/AP Images, 95; David Madison/Getty Images Sport/Getty Images, 97; Timothy A. Clary/AFP/Getty Images, 98; Jamie Squire/Getty Images Sport/Getty Images, 99; Debby Wong/Shutterstock Images, 100, 125; Ed Zurga/AP Images, 101; Jeff Kowalsky/AFP/Getty Images, 104; Jerry Holt/Star Tribune/Getty Images, 108; Focus on Sport/Getty Images, 112; David Durochik/AP Images, 113; Tim Culek/Getty Images Sport/Getty Images, 114; Bill Kostroun/AP Images, 115; Rob Brown/Getty Images Sport/Getty Images, 118; Eric Gay/AP Images, 119; Amy Sancetta/AP Images, 121